THE FURTHER ADVENTURES
OF THE LIVES OF THE SAINTS

Patrick Mackie lives in Gloucestershire.

PATRICK MACKIE

∾

The Further Adventures
Of The Lives Of The Saints

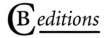

First published in Great Britain in 2016
by CB editions
146 Percy Road London W12 9QL
www.cbeditions.com

Printed in England by Blissetts, London W3 8DH

ISBN 978–1–909585–14–0

Contents

The Further Adventures
Of The Lives Of The Saints

A Holiday In The Same Place

Summer is hitting Gloucestershire like starlight spitting at a black slab of
     cloud.
The fields are not really made of greenness, it is the colour of steel or a
     seabed.
Maybe you will be able to dig down into Gloucestershire as if it was a page
     to be turned,
a grey slab to be opened,
if you can talk about a page being opened.
The grass is the colour of grass in the evenings in Africa or just outside
     Portland,
or the colour of grass in a book about techniques of warfare,
or it is grey in the slight darkness like the cover of the book or a diamond
stuck
inside a mountain.
Someone really ought to get on with dynamiting that mountain.
You have even less time than you think you do, however much of a
     mountain you are.
You should read something about logic and then maybe a few poems
about wolves.
The poets in Gloucestershire mainly like to name the riffling weeds in the
     streams.
A page in a guidebook tears itself open and the landscape is beneath,
and then the landscape tears itself open to show the shards of its grass and
     leaves,
the leaves that chatter sharply like teeth
on the muttering
branches where all the movements also withdraw themselves.
Gloucestershire is a wolf or it is a wolf to itself.
The spiders jet up into the clouds, and they look down at the fields just as
     you
can look down at the sharp silver strands that they leave behind,
the patterns that they make out of their own innards.
The spiders move within air that is murky and at the same time silvery.

The wolf is the colour of grass and it gnaws at its own bones,
not because it is trapped but because it is a wolf and hungry.
If it could it would eat itself, and then leave a generous tip.
Inside itself it would finally tell the hollow truth about Gloucestershire.
The disaster is here if it is anywhere, but at least here you can try to lie
a bit less urgently than elsewhere and more creatively too, or you can write
    poems
instead, always, one after another,
poems that eat each other and then themselves,
and then howl the truth about poetry inside themselves,
while the sun hangs on the horizon like a dazzling tooth;
it is biting someone else's lip.
On the harsh branches the birds sing about how pretty death is, or how
    appalling
beauty is,
how it comes out of poverty and flicks back into it,
hardly pausing to dazzle you on the way,
a feather writing in black ink on the black fields, and hoping that one type
    of blackness
is more shiny than the others,
lighter.
Gloucestershire is a spider and the grass is its web
in the early morning dew, the scintillating rags of its greyness.
In Gloucestershire the edge of a black barn is growing out of some pale
    nettles.
White rust has scribbled itself in bits across the corrugations of blackness,
and the white flowers of the nettles sing in the air like the
brief pale bobbles on a wrist that has got itself stung.
If happiness is not here it is nowhere, Gloucestershire is muttering,
as its tears slide down a tight black road one by one.
Gloucestershire is a window through which a hissing radio can be heard;
it is casting the slow music out as if it was a rag.
The river Rhine is flowing through Gloucestershire like a feather
flowing down the small white waves that open into a torrent.
The pale black roads tear through Gloucestershire like thorns.
Gloucestershire is flowing down the Rhine as if down a ragged
    mountainside;

a grey feather lies in a field beside a wolf's tooth.
In the joke a magical tractor turns into a field.
But right now,
you are ravished as much by your disenchantments as anything.

A Very Short Essay About The Sun

I spent a very brief part of an evening
years ago
in the house of a married couple somewhere in south Warwickshire,
around where the accents start to change if you are driving
up from Gloucestershire.
The house had once been a chapel.
It had high ceilings and a sort of rigid metallic cleanness
hovering.
So I sat amongst cushions that were white and nervous.
The strictness of light stood in piles.
Maybe I would have drunk a very small glass of vodka,
in order to be sociable or polite.
I am not sure either whether it was
on the same evening that I stopped off
at a small funfair in a town nearby,
and did rather well on
one of those machines where you try to nudge piles of coins into falling.
Years later, the husband stabbed the wife and killed her,
or at least so I heard.
The sun is a white spider, metallic, burning.

Dante

Summer can turn into a labyrinth,
a series of sweltering rooms leading off into one another,
something that you cannot see beyond,
rowan berries are flaring in the margins with a certain grim but lurid
   vehemence,
their rough orange shades are both brash and abstruse,
and in the fields greenness first flared and then found that it had burned
   itself,
now it stares into the eyes of the afternoon as if it is dazed or drunk,
or crazy,
it does not quite know who it is any longer,
puddles of brown light cluster around the base of a beech tree's sheer
   reticence,
a city is a retina flooded with slow bright greyness,
it keeps on calling anger assiduousness,
while the only calm that it knows is a servile despair,
so instead be grateful out here for a small road's graciousness,
and for the cool persistence with which it follows
the ideas of the hill's harsh bones,
it is as probing and tender as a stream or a dragonfly,
as careworn and multiform as the face of a donkey,
it is as calmly scintillating as the style of Dante,
who in any case is still walking along somewhere ahead of you;
we are poured into our precious bodies like bursts
of soft rain reworking the harsh faces of rivers,
and we must learn so many times that we do not know what to say or where
   to go.

A Quick Guide To What Being Immortal Means

If man was merely composed of dust and blood in
the end, as we keep on being told while we travel
through nervous forests
or gaze at the savage screens,
it would mean that our bodies were rivers
tearing apart their own flesh pointlessly
as they try to make themselves amount to something or go somewhere. Two
of us once got into a conversation in
the street with a man who claimed
to have found what he said was an
elixir of immortality,
and who said that he would let us
drink some of it with him if we wanted,
he was a small blunt man with a look of
something like levity scribbled on hard bland features,
but when we agreed to try it, jokingly,
or at least so we thought, he brought
his mouth down suddenly onto the inside of his right wrist,
and bit into the thin pale flesh there so
fiercely that it was all that we could do
to get him to stop before he started bleeding,
and it was unclear whether this was how
he had wanted us to react all along,
or whether he was genuinely disappointed not to be
bringing us into eternity with him,
tooth marks were etched in bright white
shades on his dull pink wrist like little waves,
but then eternity should indeed not be thought of as
a sort of straight line stretching off with no ending,
no, it lives in the ways in which each moment
strains with indelibility,
as if the river inside each one was made of rocks.

Junction

A pink shaded car rises up into the pink shades or strips of the sky.
The top of the road flickers or jumps with the small wildness of an
insect's wings.
Gustav Mahler's hands are inside your head or at least inside your hearing.
All day soldiers have been scrambling across television screens,
a long way away and also wherever anyone wants to see it.
The joke goes that a fairly dangerous intersection around here should be
    called
the extreme junction.
Light is folded in the late sky like a slow ear,
it crumples serenely,
but then it is moving too across the dirt like a small voice across the
    scuzziness of words.
It glances at the sides of the cars as they die.
It is inside your eye looking out.

A Few Spots Of Rain At The Petrol Station

You probably think that this sentence is a bit vague.
A lot of things happened by which we now feel betrayed,
while the last houses of London are beating against the fields like waves.
The roads are flowing out of the city like rivers too well behaved
to cast off the mild blackness of their own shades.
The green gleams from the traffic lights spin in the grey air like slight manes.
You can stand like the last badger on a heath or instead like a baying
hound, as it catches the light in its dark voice, and surveys
the shifting bracken in which it knows a carcass plays.
No one knows all the different words that can mean dismay,
so no one can tell you what to do with the stupidly zooming ray
in your brain that moves ahead seeking something that has not yet been
    flayed,
though the taxi drivers and policemen between them know who can be saved
and who consigned to the restful heap of those who forgot to crave.
We stood in line at the popcorn stands as if we were each other's slaves.
Now the budget hotel stands with its mouth swung open as if amazed.
The lines of cars on the roundabout hiss and wind like broken snakes,
and autumn has fallen on the fidgeting branches and shrubs like a slow razor.
The year is lurching and sliding like a comedian learning to skate,
and the leaves drag as the winter takes little bits out of their shapes,
but it was so nearly enough to be so smoothly entertained,
if the others could die elsewhere, if their deaths were kept on other pages,
while the radio stations whispered and the sky obliged, obeyed,
so now water scuttles down the slick sinks, as if it too feels betrayed.
Sliding doors whir open and closed in front of the bright displays,
as blank as if they believed that there was no one who could not pay.
We swallowed money as briskly as if it was grain or rain or flames.
The darkness was always getting ready to spit out another day.
Now the sky says 'crow' and 'crow' and then 'cloud' until the sunshine is
    slain,
and the face of Venus sets fire to itself and wears its brightness as a stain,
and Orion lifts his vague burning arms to show that even he is afraid.

The city keeps spitting out light as if it is trying to make something clear,
but then like any other immigrant it is made of doubts and fears.
Petrol slips around the pumps as if it was the ground's idea of tears,
and a siren cuts up the dark air, and then aches, and then disappears,
leaving the moments to try to repeat themselves in each car's mirrors.
The night will wash in blackness everything that the day smeared.
A black cat drifts to a window and launches its metallic stare,
and looks as if it could explain why utopia means nowhere.
But nothing is really obscure in these words, except what you want to say.
It might have been better if someone like Hölderlin could have been here
     today,
to tell us that there was some deep abyss within the shallow array,
in lines that would have flowed like water that was turning into a prayer.
But the years kept rushing as steeply as if they were built like drains,
and no one knew the difference between a plague and a brash aim.
The hills are grey and harsh now as they scratch like nails or like blame.

A Brief And Helpless Treatise On The Subject Of The Heart

The tender evening light carried on shifting like a batch of hazy pigeons from
 rooftop
to rooftop before it finally settled. The charred shapes
of the colonnade, if that is the right word for it, breathed
calmly. I was waiting while a friend spoke
on the telephone to some colleagues and officials,
all of them trying to decide whether one of
her students should be committed or not to
a mental hospital. A few stars were nailing some thin clouds to the pale grey
 sky,
the weak teeth of the ivy whirred in the greyness,
and spoke. But they spoke in a foreign language. We are so
accustomed to so much failure when we attempt
to look into the minds of others that it is
all the more startling and frightening when we
abruptly succeed. Knowledge moved like a mist in the empty air,
so ashen and serene and comfortless,
a face on which the bright colours had burned themselves out. A library was
floating and whispering up above me, students were leaving
notes on coloured bits of paper in
their tiring copies of the same old tremendous classics,
beyond it roads stepped slowly away like yet more rough black thoughts trying
to inch away from themselves without anyone
noticing. The heart has no wings because it is a wing itself,
a single wing beating within the weakness of the flesh like a lake within its
 breaking
reflections, streaming as if it wanted to be able to
mount back up through the steep air like snow moving backwards
so as to throw its spreading shades back into their white beginnings. If
it should find another wing though,
it may be able to fly. Nearby,
a lake was rising out of itself like a tremulous grey eye.
I believe that this poem wants to be the reason why.

In Memory Of Alexander Vvedensky

I begin this poem walking with him through a wildly grey February day.
He is resting there in my bag like a small lion at bay,
and then he opens his mouth as if he could swallow a whole bay.
We are in London and it is waiting for an election like a human
cannonball waiting inside a cannon for days on end.
The audience went home weeks ago and in any case will not
admit that it does not really want much to change.
Unbelievably various heaps of grey light stand amongst the buildings
and trees and hoardings and grocery crates and defunct telephone boxes
    and railings,
and watch us.
Vvedensky turns and says to me that the sea has no meaning.
He says that the future shot time dead a long time ago,
although it may have died of dysentery instead.
He says that time is a clock with a face that he
painted over with his own cracked face a long time ago,
because he was afraid and wonderful.
I tell him that I want to be afraid and wonderful too.
We rail and dissent and so does everyone else and so do you.
Nothing looks true but the truth is that nothing is untrue,
not the beech tree with the face of a lizard,
not the streams of messages that wander in the streets like lost pain or
    shoals of starlight.
Vvedensky says that there are always two rhythms when you are
writing, a good one and a bad one,
and that you should always choose the bad one.
But then London turns its face to me too and says the exact same thing.
Why did the twentieth century so often end up
equating train stations with death?
I watch,
and he is reading about it all in his own quick poems,
and the time is a century ago and then it is now.

Early Mandelstam

Tough little angels of sound are howling off the rich surfaces of the water
    tonight,
but do not let that worry you.
The river Avon is bright black and yet it is not worried.
Harsh little ripples of what is not in fact cold sweat lick and etch around
the edges as it goes bending and loosening downwards.
It is covered in fragments of speed moving in bright little twitches and
    gurgles.
All the sounds rush towards it as if they had just discovered thirst,
and then they skid off it because it is too dark to drink.
Its water is as suave and tough as a piano lid.
I have got the early Mandelstam blues bending in my brain.
The tunes are hard and quiet and permanent like the veins
stretched taut across the body of a small wet stone.
Mandelstam translated some of my best things into Russian a century or so
    ago,
and of course this was quite an honour for me,
though he should perhaps have waited for me to write them first.
It will just look like copying if I write them now.
The nighttime is turning the day into a foreign language now,
a language that at least is equally foreign to us all,
one that breaks all the splendid syllables down into pieces
and then flings them over the pale buildings
as if description had been a bad idea in the first place.
The day is washing its face off in the wet black air.
Streetlights are wandering around on the vanishing slopes,
and getting older too seems to mean getting weirder and weirder by the day.
I have not been in an aeroplane for well over a decade,
and this is just a single example for you.
The revolution came and ate up all its poets as if they were merely sounds or
    moths
or starlight.
All the buildings here stand as still as ghosts that are frightened of
    themselves.

I am very slowly turning into water vapour.
I guess that it is one way of being
translated,
while the softness of the stone bridge still reaches and wavers like a tongue.

A Hymn That Is Made Of Butter

The Sanskrit hymn describing holy butter that this is a loose and ignorant
version of begins with a sort of flowing
sweetness like a slow wave of honey,
a wave rising up from the ocean and then fusing
itself with the thread that contains the juice of life and so creating
something immortal,
and the whole reason why this butter is so holy is this fusion stirring deep
    within it.
So right at the heart of this butter something immortal
is whispering its secrets right at the edge of speech.
But this is why we should say the name of butter aloud,
and hold the butter up in the clear blue air as an offering,
at the same time as we bow low.
We should say its name loud and clear so that the priests hear it.
First there was a great buffalo with four vast horns,
and then all this butter came gushing out of it.
The butter raced away from the buffalo's four horns,
and its three feet and its two heads and its seven hands.
First a great bull was held down with three vast bindings,
and now you can hear the sweet violence of its cry.
Something immortal must be tearing its way into death.
All this butter was once held within a single cow,
and that indeed was where the immortals discovered it,
the butter whose parts had in fact been hidden there by our enemies.
But the king lifted a part out and the sun also lifted a part out,
and together they restored the final part to its own shape,
using the flames of their own desires to shape it.
So now streams of butter are flowing from the heart of the ocean,
and they are guided in a hundred channels,
and none of the bad guys can see them at all.
I can still watch the rapture of their course though,
and I can see the reed made of gold that is guiding them onwards.
So too these words join like rivers that flow together,

and they are cleaned by the knowledge held deep in the heart.
Waves of butter flow like deer that are coursing from an archer.
Fresh streams of butter surge like the whips in a river's torrents,
rising up and then swelling with waves like quick mazes,
accelerating past the wind like a bright chestnut racehorse
as it breaks right through
all the tracks that are laid out for racehorses to stream in.
The streams of butter zoom off to find the immortal flames,
and they smile as they do so like beautiful women streaming to a festival.
The butter touches the burning wood and the brightness of the fire kisses it.
As I watch these streams they seem like young women anointing
themselves with little streams of perfumed oil before going to a
wedding.
So wherever the juice of life lifts and gushes,
and the fire of a sacrifice is flowing with flames,
it is there that these streams quicken on into brightness and clarity.
So let us let loose the waves of a hymn now too,
and let us hold races with amazing cows as prizes.
Let all the bright objects in the world come shining towards us.
Let us hope that our sacrifice flows all the way to the immortals,
now that the sweet streams of butter have made things so blindingly bright,
so clear.
The whole world has brightened in the centre of your being,
and it stirs within the ocean and the heart,
and the years in which you are ignorant yet alive.
All that we want is to grasp these mellifluous streams,
to ride on their waves until we arrive where they bring us,
the place where the faces of the waters all leap into one.

Reflection

No one could be less frightened than the mist at being so alone.
So it shakes its soft bright bones.

A Short History Of The Second World War

My grandfather flew a fighter made largely of wood and stopped Hitler from
     invading,
and then decades later he and my grandmother
divorced,
a rare thing still in those days in their set,
their marriage having foundered because he drank,
although possibly from the start they were also badly
matched,
and had only met and fallen in love or, at least, fallen
together because of the war and all the excitement and fear and
     displacement,
so later he moved to somewhere in East Anglia where I for one never visited,
somewhere by the marshy coast,
somewhere where he could carry on drinking, happily
enough, possibly,
wound right inside the solid grey weather of postwar history,
as its governments came and went like fairly empty coaches on minor roads,
my grandmother once told me that she had the only migraine of her life on
     their
wedding night,
right in the middle of the war, somewhere
in a hotel placed carefully down in the rural southwest,
all across the countryside people had turned road signs the wrong
way round, to confuse anyone who did invade,
night air slept on the empty lanes like a beggar in ecstasy,
and she lay awake and heard him carrying on, as she would put it,
at the bar downstairs late into the black night,
but then all of us have fallen from the sky, whether bleakly or slowly or
     headily,
and we whisper and stare upwards like undulating roads on stark nights.

In Praise Of The Black Coast

Steven Spielberg is shooting the opening minutes
of *Jaws* over and over again on a dark beach,
or at least this is how you imagine it, he stands
watching as a young couple breaks off from a party,
and she announces that she is going to go
swimming, the sea waits with its big black mouth
hanging open like the coolness of history,
and Spielberg turns to the orchestra that is
waiting there beside him amongst the dim dunes,
and over and over again you hear the gorgeously
low growl of those rhythms start up in the strings,
as you have heard it innumerable times in
the intervening years,
he is getting ready to scare the hell out
of us all, it is not much more than thirty
years since the death camps in Europe,
and now Ronald Reagan too is getting himself
ready, by the end of the decade he will be
drifting into the White House like a shark's grey fin,
the ocean is whirring its cameras, the shark
is getting ready for its big number,
the director in fact feels himself beginning to
cry, but then Hollywood itself has died so often
too, killed by television and video and the internet,
and now indeed the poem alone remains standing
on the beach, gazing slowly into the viewfinder,
and then turning away to write its own black name in
the veins of the waves of the sea.

On Ghosts

In the end the joke was on the ghosts,
as they haunted the empty rooms night after night.

Adlestrop

Hefty beige stretches of moonlight are smeared on the dark chestnut head
    of the
horse,
as you try to lead it back into what you hope is the correct field
at around two in the morning in the moist summer night,
it had appeared in front of your car,
rising up suddenly,
a staggering head in the speed of the headlights,
and then a body like a low brown cloud,
right in the middle of the road that goes streaming along the edge of the
    village,
and, yes, it is the same small village where the express train drew up
restlessly a century or so ago,
and where a poet drew what sounds and meanings he could
out from the bright little lapse that time had made in itself,
and then he was dead not many years afterwards,
and now he seems to have reappeared in the spirited guise
of a horse to make you stop here in the wide open night,
strong, probably a racehorse, but with gentle eyes that are now slightly
    bewildered,
you could have killed the horse or it could have killed you,
but now you have parked your car and you are talking it through
the shimmering and soft wooden gate into the airy field,
its breath is warm and quietly noisy in the moist moonlight,
and the night is a word inside a dark mouth and it too really wants to
    speak.

Arcturus

Stunningly awake and unbelievably emotional and possibly a little cruel,
but only so that it can see
you more entirely,
after all the years in which you did not know where or
possibly what it
was, now it speaks like a chariot,
it stares like one too,
it throws wild force and beauty into a single song or
reckoning like the face of a passerby nailing itself into the
memory with a single stroke of genius,
its thoughts are climbing like stairs,
and rough little colours of flame do seem to imbue
the nineteen million miles or so that it is meant to measure across,
though it is hard to know how far to trust that sort of
feeling,
while the universe shimmers as bleakly as tar
and cruises with its mouth dangling open like a rusty
whale, swallowing its own edges one by one,
unbelievable quantities of black nothingness hang up there on top of
the dark air,
but the star will not leave you for a while,
and owls keep leaving the little black flowers of their songs amidst the
    branches,
to watch over all the other things that you are interested in, the drifting
ghost of a stone wall or a small road roaming like an eye.

Cassiopeia

A letter that was not even in her alphabet
is spelling her out now endlessly as she wheels,
something that happens
to any number of women sooner or later,
she is thus wonderful and wistful,
or she is witty and waylaid and
wasted, now there are tough wisps of
cirrus touching her, and now
the stars are dying in her hair like dew
seeping into moss amidst slender dark branches,
and you search the sky for goodness and find nuclear explosions,
and in fact that is one of the things that goodness is.

Branch

Sometimes you fall so far down into sleep that it feels as if sleep is itself
asleep, it lies beside you with one warm arm
wreathed lightly across
you, but it keeps its face turned away from you, and when you
do wake up, you also stay shyly asleep,
the world is still covered
too with so much sleep that its flesh is like fine dust only held together
by slowness, but then sleep is waiting every day
inside you anyway like a pear inside
a branch, it is the colour of the eyes of moths but it takes its sounds from the
erratic memories of small harbours at night,
it swims down inside itself
as patiently as the moonlight drifting on the swimming pool in a small
 garden,
the guests mostly went home quietly drunk,
and now the flowers are washing
themselves in so much darkness that even the air only knows them by
touch; you see someone sleeping and you do not know if it
is the ultimate in flesh or in spirit.

The Neighbours

In René Char's country it was all translation in the first place, and also primeval. In his country you dream that the houses have no windowpanes. His country is one where sand is a bittersweet friend. Footpaths covered with sleeping herbs lead away from a village called Thor which plays on the lyre of its rocks. In Char's country a meadow encases the day. In our country an endlessly sharp swallow sings in a sky so grey that it is otherwise empty. A stream is a torch which leads us to dormant lakes. In your country the moon in a lake takes a single step onto the beach where the soft fire of strands of grass is walking down into the water. War too is being declared here deep within the slabs of sky hidden beneath the rock faces. So we live in a country where no one understands much at all, and where the eye screws itself up as early as it can. So in his country gratitude may just save your skin or at least your heart. In your country the dawn turns people into strangers. The storms are so transparent in our country that they take you right into the hills of our spirits. We will see him there from time to time before he turns again quickly and solidly into his blank brain.

A Tongue

The woods here are giving you a different voice every day,
one day it is richly damp while the rain on the leaves
and tangled branches flows in and out of it,
another day it is thinned out by fine solutions of sunlight,
and another day it is given grounding and thickness
by the slow grey layers of air that have been slowed down themselves
by the thick leaves layered amongst some roots or on the rutted paths,
it is like being a ventriloquist's dummy except that you are walking around,
you have a wooden tongue, of course,
and you often catch sight of a deer catching sight of you briefly
at the time of day when the day is peeling
itself back to show the evening that waits inside it,
as if it was a seared leaf falling from a branch,
and it may be that the deer is a falling leaf too
as it crumbles back into the grey trees and the darkness of the light,
but it did at least show you its immortality briefly,
nervously,
its speed is one of the forms that eternity takes,
as if its body was a word spoken by the wood's sweetest voice,
a colour burning on the wood's tongue briefly and
forever,
in the middle of the margins of the world's rough flames;
beauty is egalitarian.

A Little Statue Of Krishna

Hi, wisdom,
you have presumably come yet again to show us
the night sky, and a big hello to you
too, Clotho, the evening has indeed succeeded
in grinding itself down into dust yet again and then thrown
the dust over its shoulder and watched it turn into starlight,
and your sister has brought her shiniest pair of scissors,
our warmest greetings also to the ghost
of Yannis Ritsos, he looks up, and the sky
is full of hunters and beasts stalking one another,
as if language and murder had always overlapped,
the last fragments of the wind are circling like little blind
wings, and now Jackson Pollock has come to trace
white dashes on the high walls of the darkness,
he is as beautiful as a cave himself, and we watch,
as one star shoots another star down in flames,
and another star sinks its sharp
white teeth into another star's gleaming thighs,
and another star drinks in the heat of another star's glare,
inside each human hand there is a cobra,
and statecraft turns into a way of drinking rivers
dry, and marriages turn out to be ways of trying
to keep secrets or at best of keeping secrets fresh,
but now comes, finally, the memory of a tiny golden statue
of the nonexistent god Krishna playing his flute,
amidst the void on a museum shelf.

Wyoming

Sometimes these thoughts will go roaming off to where whatever happened
    to you
happened,
the places where you disappeared from sight,
places where I never visited you,
in fact where I have never been at all,
but I picture bluffs and black lakes and vast skies that go
roaming some days and then the next are devastatingly still and grey and
    witless,
headlights wandering along crazily long highways,
all these vistas that come walking in from postcards or mediocre films,
the sun in winter spitting cold lines of light like a bad headache,
I liked you so much and knew you so little really,
maybe I should say that I loved you but I do not really know how
    trustworthy
it would be,
and my thoughts come back every time from there without you.

The People Who Live On The Sun

The people who live on the sun are watching us through telescopes made of
    flames,
of course, since there is nothing there that is not made of
flames.
If the people who live on the sun cry,
the tears that course down their bright faces are made of flames.
Their rivers are made of flames and their swimming pools are made of flames,
and so are their fizzy drinks and their vending machines.
In their kitchens they have heat-resistant work tops made of flames.
So appearances are not deceptive when it comes to life on the sun.
Someone told the people on the sun about the Buddha's fire sermon,
and what they said was 'So what else is new?'
In their cosmology water got a fever and fire came growling out of it,
and then went eating up all the water across all the worlds.
In their version of genetics fire is a dragon that eats itself
and then breathes itself out in the form of different genes into people's chests.
In their poetics singing is just the most refined way of burning,
one that reveals the many ways in which flames can
coruscate and enlighten and then whisper.
Because they cannot see us during our nights, their belief
is that we turn back into water when sleep takes us,
and awake only on recalling that water no longer exists.
The moon from their point of view is just a big slow spark.
In their dreams they are fish at the centre of a planet made of water,
but then what floods them when they wake up is guilt.
The people there who study us most closely have concluded that we
are flames too, of course, but burning at a much lower pitch.
Now some of them are even saying that it is cruel
to leave us floundering out here where the fire is so slight and dim,
and that they really ought to send off some sort of mission to rescue us.
You might say that this is mere solar demagoguery.
But their assemblies debate diagrams that show a fiery hand reaching out
of the sun and down through the cold black flame of space to us,
so that they can bring us in and at long last heal us.

One Car

One car roars huskily amidst the blur of the night,
one car drifts on a lake of moonlight. One car
is eating clusters of bright rain in large gulps. One car
stretches its neck out like a duck in flight, one car
listens to songs from the first days of disco. One car thirsts,
one car meditates, one car seems calm but in fact it is
filled with pain that no one can understand. One car hates
you but it is not the one that you think. One car
paints skilful if rather splashy watercolours of
the passing landscapes on its windscreen.
One car howls and one car rusts and one car dreams
of war. One car is trying to pass itself off
as another car, but then sometimes this is a way of finding out
who you really are in the first place. One car floats and one car loves all
animals, in ways that strike other cars as both squalid and
graceful. In one car two people are making a home for themselves,
while one car looks as if it has been forever
empty. One car is stuck in the past like a bad
newspaper article. One car has not read its own
instruction manual. One car is shredded with fear and one car
hustles. One car keeps whispering into the evening haze as if
the road was a place to pray in, or at least to be honest in,
a place where each car matters and has something drastic to say.

How To Avoid Being Eaten By An Owl

The owl was so far inside itself that all that you could see
was the fire of its disappearance on the white air,
the air dizzied into whiteness,
the stomach of the air wheeling and choking,
the owl dropping like a little block of vertigo up into the pupil of the air,
stamping its feet on the high cinders of the ground of the sky,
the air spat its own blackness back out all over itself,
the whites of its eyes were closing,
and the owl had ended up committing suicide,
or it had told some grim jokes then soared off stage to great but rather cold
    applause,
it had built the moon by flying straight into a large rough stone,
and it sat there now inside your head like the white curve of a limb broken
    from an
irresistible statue,
burning,
while the little white claws of the stars scratched away at the empty head of the
night;
she had dropped away from you too, but she was also still standing in front of
    you,
holding the pallor of her body in the dark palms of her
hands.

A Short Essay on the Ethics of Leaves

Brisk, undoing itself, the wind is making little circles of fire at the ends of
  the leaves;
another wind bit down into the day, chewed it down to its remnants,
but now the tough brightness of the edges of the ash tree's leaves
is claiming that they still hold storms of light inside themselves,
while one of the ghosts of Bertolt Brecht walks sharply past the garden,
  reading
the newspaper upside down because he does not want to understand it,
but whistling songs that he claims have still not yet been written.

In Memory Of The Work Of Italo Calvino

I want to tell you a story about
a story. A story went out walking in the
strong doubtful forest. Another story walked amidst a shining
crowd, it was handing out coins and asking
if anyone knew any good stories,
but it was last seen weeping to itself in
the slurred light of a stairwell. Yet another story
was seen leaping onto the shiny back of
a tiger. It may not have been a tiger,
but something no less angry like a river or a city instead,
something sharp. Nothing more was heard until some years later,
and even then the reports could not be trusted. The story
had last been seen in tatters at the edge of a forest,
or at least so we heard,
or it was stranded against the teeth of a pale yellow horizon, or it had
escaped by turning into a story in a different tradition,
one about a cloud dwelling on the top of a sharp mountain,
and learning to speak in that hard air. The mountain
had the face of a tiger. The crowds
had flowed off into the sea countless
years ago, and the forest was seen weeping by the sides
of the rivers that are always leaping on the back of the earth,
and its tears assumed the savage brown shapes
of autumn. I want the landscape to roam like an ear. His
stories went off journeying one by one,
in search of the light red city of justice. The days are
so precious and light now too though that no matter how quickly I chase
after them or how nimbly,
it is like chasing after the hard blue sun glazed
on a piece of china that is falling and breaking,
and nothing can be finally caught in a world whereby
stillness and speed are so deftly and richly mixed.

Athena

Traffic never seems to know what it is doing,
but the truth is that you are part of it. The late afternoon
was layering blasts of low sunlight on the smears of your windscreen,
as if light wanted to show how blind it can be. Lorries
raged like smoke over the entranced lines of the roads. The faces
of people while they drive are as mysterious as
the feet of swans and as dumb as water. Names of towns
drifted past but then repeated themselves as if they could
not think of anything else to say. Later,
you were at the supermarket checkout buying some pizzas
and so on, while the woman working the till began to tell you how
she was planning to see a psychic the next evening,
a friend with an interest in the supernatural had found one,
and she was going to try to reach her recently deceased mother,
or rather, the way that she put it was that she wanted her mother
to come through. A room in a pub had been organised,
and supper would be included in the price. Outside,
night had fallen as casually as leaves into a dark stream.
In the car park the air had a sweet dusty tang like cinnamon. You
do still believe in the muses at least sometimes,
or rather in the forces that they can still be the names for,
and so too sometimes in Athena with her mind made of flames,
and her eyes that are as cool and liquid as snakes,
and always in the spirit as it dives into the cold fire of each day,
but then swims like fierce moonlight on the even wilder surfaces of the
    night.

Amanuensis

Somebody is sailing a small dark boat on a
sea of death which you cannot see any longer,
and so now the only thing that you can do is to listen
to the boat that is still moving on it,
the rhythms that cloud and then stretch or brighten like lakes,
and of course the grand piano is open like a sail too,
frail ribbons of light are moving in slow gusts across its hoisted darkness,
maybe it is pain that is walking towards you on the full air,
the stupefied air,
but when it reaches you its face is made of the cool dim air of music.

To Franz Rosenzweig

Franz Rosenzweig watched the trenches and craters and explosions,
and the word that he wrote was 'creation'. He watched
a wound burning slowly on a face and out of it
he drew the word 'redemption'. Of course,
you do not have to believe him. The cover
photograph makes him look oddly like Trotsky. He
would be unworldly in his air of silvery distraction,
except that the ardency is sharp enough to hurt anyone.
Sallow, fragile, permanent,
he is handing you the book that he was writing,
as if you were his neighbour after all, and capable of being loved.

In Memory Of Amy Winehouse

Hot weather in London quickly feels bizarrely
natural. It was my first evening at the
swanky flat near Oxford Street which my then new
girlfriend was renting. The soft air
was hazy or even slightly heavy with happiness
as we walked round the neighbourhood. We
got together for a while and then broke up,
and got back together and later broke up completely. But
all of this was some time ago now. At the top
of the street amongst drifts of late evening warmth,
we saw Amy Winehouse standing there with a cigarette.
She looked tiny and sumptuous and slightly lost at the edge of
a small group of softly talking friends. She
looked in fact to me like poetry summed up, so lavish
but at the same time so starkly factual. Her black
voice sat inside her and watched the future go
by with its warm hands full of shadows.

Frontline

Another small war was just ending or maybe one was just starting,
or maybe it was the same one, and nobody knew any longer
how to tell the end of a war from the start of one,
the evening news programmes swam like bright planets,
but looked about as far away too,
web pages whirred as fiercely as midges,
across the world opinions shimmered and groaned like the noise of a
    fridge,
and you had ended up taking a lot of ibuprofen as normal,
headlights darted fastidiously on the dim hillsides,
but then the moon was coming up too,
the moon that can never be either normal or strange,
throwing her first slender thoughts amongst the faltering beech trees and
    the vague
tatters of the telephone wires,
her wild thoughts that always clothe themselves in mild little shocks of
    radiance,
the moon that is both gentle and, endlessly, a huntress,
arching above the faintly lacerated earth,
while its shapes hold their breaths in the darkness and the night breathes
    out;
we need to find ways of hunting that are gentle,
forms of peace that are as accurate and sharp as arrows can be.

Slide

We cried.
Twilight walked up to the city like a vast and sulky bride.
We cried.
The sky went through some miserable colours and then fried.
We cried.
In the end the trouble with politicians is not that they have not tried,
it is the fact that they too are mystified.
We cried.
All the coffee chains mixed and fought like Etruscan tribes
in the grey air which lifted up from the pavements like steam or like pride.
We cried.
The ambulances were taking sick people for rides.
We cried.
In offices the share prices still shook with fear or smiled,
or writhed.
We cried.
One man fears what he derides,
another one loves something even more if it gives him a chance to be snide.
We cried.
Police vans slid open their doors to show that nothing worth taking was
        inside,
and newspapers slid from hand to hand in the dusk like flies.
We cried.
One street was dressed in a tuxedo, but we spied
other streets wandering off dressed in rags or in hides,
and others wearing only enormous necklaces, and looking not exactly
        dignified.
We cried.
In the street of maxed out credit cards nothing was now undenied,
but the mannequins still stared lovingly down at the bus stops waiting
        outside.
We cried.
In the street of snake skins the air was as tasteless as cyanide.
We cried.

The global banking system does not care how many trades you have plied,
or how much sympathy its own tears describe.
We cried.
Someone was planning a seminar on the subject of genocide,
and someone else was thinking of calling a punk revival band Suicide.
We cried.
Our tears made us feel a bit more satisfied.
We cried.
In the street of charity all the passersby were helplessly allied.
We cried.
In the street of glass the air fell from an enormous height,
and then looked at you as vacantly as a prisoner whom you have just
    untied.
We cried.
The street of cameras was filled with stubbornly ignorant guides.
We cried.
The backs of small houses were watching one another like pensioners at the
    seaside.
We cried.
A cold breeze slowly chewed on all the tough little flecks of carbon
    monoxide.
We cried.
The police horses reared slightly and shied,
and the dusk waited outside the betting shops with its jaws open like a
    termite.
We cried.
Sitting rooms were filled with starry dramas about the city's mean
    underside.
We cried.
In fact pity and pornography have both become extravagantly rarefied.
We cried.
In the street of lubricious glances moral lessons were also supplied,
and they came and went like tides.
We cried.
In the street of snails there was no override
button, so we kept ending up stuck with the broken shells and the
    bromides.

We cried.

In the street of reversals the cars sat glumly and waited for the night,
unable to stampede even when the noise made them terrified.

We cried.

Barmen and baristas smiled madly to prove that they were not tired,
and someone advertised a job for which two and a half million people
straightaway applied.

We cried.

Pub doors whirred open and shut like breathtaking yawns and, besides,
people do seem to like to collide.

We cried.

We admired,
of course, how profusely the tattoos on the forearms of footballers
multiplied.

We cried.

We lied and grew wide and committed symbolic parricide,
and our favourite songs had relentless beats that only seemed to chide.

We cried.

The parking rules kept changing but we still mainly complied,
and our communications systems heard each message and replied,
so that not even the smallest or the most reprehensible whisper would ever
subside.

We cried.

It was hard to tell what was a perfume and what an oddly fragrant
spermicide.

We cried.

The past was merely inept like a dead newspaper at the roadside.

We cried.

The air was a crumpled ball of paper on which our details had once been
inscribed,
but now there were only sums involving proportions of carbon dioxide.

We cried.

By constrast, the new flavours of ice cream had names that were inspired.

We cried.

The greedy and the promiscuous and the desperate and the beguiled,
and the people with nowhere to reside,
all sighed.

We cried.
The low moon stood on the backs of the fast clouds and waterskied.
We cried.
Darkness seeped out of the office blocks as if they were being slowly
    liquefied.
We cried.
Not even the smartest critical theorists could avoid feeling a bit reified,
on seeing so many posters featuring such fabulous backsides.
We cried.
A dumb grey crossed with righteous anger is the colour of the city's id.
We cried.
But satnav entrepeneurs generously promised to provide
all the facts about our own homes that the estate agents had whisked aside.
We cried.
The best of us looked as glamorous and as stupid as Bonnie and Clyde.
We cried.
We died and then woke up again as often as the entertainment required.
We cried.
Now the night was getting ready to take one huge and meticulous stride.
We cried.
At the last minute slumber ramified,
and it opened its soft black heart like a slide.

The Dew Will Make No Comment

As if the day needs to weep before it can properly begin,
or like fizzy water turned inside
out, and slowed
right down too, simmering amidst the seas of grass like the
fading scars of tiny burns, clingy little dollops
of wet light,
scooped out of the flowing dreams that normally still hold you
at this point, and then poured back down jot by
jot onto the hungry world,
so polished but also so oblique, halfway between blandness and tension like
    pigeon
feathers or like the shapeliness of a
rifle, vestiges holding
on tight to the coldness and inwardness of the nighttime,
or sharp little creatures made of the liveliest
and most tender edges of
the sun, empty thought bubbles, in fact they give away nothing
precisely, because they know that dawn can be
bizarrely splendid
one day, and then the next day waxen and even appalling.

On Interiority

The fabric was called loss but she had stitched the word stealth into it,
so that some things would not have to be lost completely.

Anthropology

He was working on something that was partly a robot and partly a novel.

～

We took breaks from each other as if time itself was hurting.

～

Who could fail to love a film like *Freaks* whose lost scenes may have included one depicting the castration of a strongman?

～

The era of Samuel Beckett has just finished; the era of Raphael and Manet is always beginning.

～

It is pointless being a Dadaist unless you are also a Christian or something like it.

～

You will be eaten up by the Dadaists unless you eat them first.

～

Cities are great in proportion to the anger that they can contain; you were just astute enough to need to be loved.

～

All the dentists marched in phalanxes by night, wondering when they would take complete control.

~

She just kept counting the departure lounges, convinced that she had made a mistake.

~

People were waiting around like complaint forms.

~

If he had been alive now instead, he might have said that you are one part of the taste of politics.

~

Charles Fourier was still a socialist as he sat on his own, clothed in his endless cities of thought; the internet does not love you as much as it claims.

~

Picasso was both the minotaur and the thread, and in fact some people can only find the thread by at least pretending to be the minotaur; she must have got bored of ravelling it out to the prince.

~

Might not your misgivings form part of the brain of injustice?

~

Robert Kennedy intoned his lines from Aeschylus in the bed beside you night after night.

~

The words have even worse shadows now, lassoed as they are in one another's glare, transfixed by feedback.

∽

A breath walks over a bridge made of air; the days are kept so strictly apart that they do not even glance at one another.

∽

The two of you watched each other like a river watching a field, so full of love but also grabbing at every dash of earth.

∽

The same swallow came in the evenings, its comments ending in small xylophones, its feathers burning coolly inside the fuel of the dark light.

∽

A bird argues in a gust and becomes a bridge; he wanted to write a sentence that would refuse to be uploaded.

∽

A folk tale went off in search of the future.

∽

The sentence was a bridge as it stood inside your eyes like the span of a mouth.

∽

Do not be unduly afraid of the radiance of Guy Debord; his insights came straight from his stubbornness, and his stubbornness came straight from his cunning which itself came straight from his helplessness.

～

At the top of all the high arguments King Kong is still teetering.

～

In the body of John Wayne, you see charm and even a fatal grace rising all of a sudden within the sheer fatalism of substance.

～

Drink lemonade poured for you by the man on the brink.

～

He was so proud to be so uncertain; in fact the self had ended up right back where it had started.

～

The ghost of Simone Weil swims down to the broken hulls like a flame inside a stone.

～

Would it be true to say that I broke my eyes on some of these stones years and years ago?

～

Did you really not know that the space between the earth and the sun is a horse on which the waves of sunlight are riding?

～

I remember a pale hand raised amongst the library buildings in a greeting that was also a severance.

～

It was John Wayne who stood there joining together the earth and the sky; you will have to get your head around it.

～

Endlessness had you by the jugular; you can choose whether to be bored or eternal.

～

The horses move in large slow jolts like wide rivers inside the moon's gawping passion, the divine life was even more sensitive than the nose of a fox.

～

You could hear all the global corporations softly weeping in the fog.

～

Now they need to leave the very concept of nature behind, amidst the footpaths that lie fallen and radiant like girders.

～

Nature was the world's largest carnivorous plant.

～

I saw Walter Benjamin dressed as Ronald McDonald.

～

In fact Kim Kardashian prefers a more conventional type of lyric.

∾

He steeped his hand in her psyche as she slept, right up to the elbow and beyond, up to the city where he had been marooned so long ago.

∾

The small owls tear holes in the quietness and pour their hard voices through.

∾

Listen to an owl and then tell me that you are not a voice with a body attached.

∾

I saw the owls cut like jewels from one edge of the night to the other; it was a good time to be an owl, patches of light had been strapped to the back of history.

∾

Events ran like mice down the throats of our political defeats.

∾

It starts with a hole and then a stomach grows around it, and then a mouth grows out of the stomach, and before long you have a howling owl.

∾

Surveillance was a desert in the first place; in fact what we need is a new populace.

∾

Fields of lightning wandered across the night in search of things to eat, you heard a sort of ointment of laughter right at the edge of the divine lines.

∽

She held her breath while she was writing, as if it would help the words to breathe instead.

∽

The letters of the alphabet sit around and laugh about us.

∽

A letter is a line that has something wrong with it; a thought is a thought that has something wrong with it.

∽

Eat beauty, and study spittle, you can hear the winds because they break like windows.

∽

The sky is a human skin stretched over us to remind us that we have lost something; it is made of oxygen and sharpened water like your brain.

∽

It will swallow you unless you teach it how to sing first.

∽

I saw a blackbird spitting out the evening in gobbets from off its little black tongue.

∽

People were waiting around later like old films.

∾

She lived in an empire made of loose departures and bright impatience
and the edges of management textbooks, an empire the shape of her own
body but also as various, she listened so forcibly in the heat of the basement
lecture theatre.

∾

We were attenuated and we loved it and our tears broke off from us like ice
stalking over a cave's lost flames.

∾

The stars of the silent age became even more silent afterwards, in fact they
hid their silence in the history of cinema, wrapped it in little silver flames
that protected you too.

∾

How many muses would you say that there are by now, if you include at
least the muses for sarcastic laughter and for bad video art, and the muses
for critical theory and for drifting horizons and for space travel?

∾

The great temptation was to turn your back on paradise, it was all the
greater because you could not really do so, in the end there are just so many
types of paradise that one of them always gets you.

∾

A crow was chewing the dusky light with the teeth inside its voice.

∾

Now people were waiting around like vaseline.

∾

Her soul kept on changing its scale, sometimes it was as small as the head of a pin, at other times it enlarged her just as the colours of the leaves jut out from a tree's syntax.

∾

The earth is thinking hard about what to do with you.

∾

Their jobs fell off them like bathwater, moodily, slickly.

∾

The television stations had taken them so far from home and even from desire.

∾

You need to let the person walk away from you amongst the street signs and the awnings, the stories are written from a certain distance, and without looking back at their faces.

∾

The letters of the alphabet are so quiet, whether out of pride or cunning or anger, or patience.

∾

Buster Keaton walked silently through the disasters with only the cunning of his innocence to protect him.

~

You could always turn to Fred Astaire and watch him dance on the very edges where black meets white.

~

Go back to Blake and tell him that we demand the return of our experiences, we demand the return of film from the era of digitization; we know that we will not get the latter.

~

The speed of eternity is what stops people from seeing it.

~

The day did not stop watching him; the name of one of its eyes was change and eternity was the name of the other.

~

On her passenger seat she carried a pillow.

~

He was dreaming harder and harder each night, as if his face had stopped trying to protect him.

~

Of course the blues will never end; you might as well ask the patience of a prayer to end.

~

Art was standing in front of him with a ball of wool held in each of its clusters of fingers, the red wool represented the heart and the black wool represented a blade, and the aim was to join them without letting either prevail.

∽

Our lives are walking close behind us, but they will not say anything to our faces.

∽

You will not change wealth if you do not redistribute sensation.

∽

Do not be too upset if democracy is sometimes sad.

∽

Did you really think that you would not be bored, sailing there at the top of the sacred mountain with your face wreathed in bullet points?

∽

The sunset had exactly the same expression as Emily Dickinson as it smeared the roofs and gables, and then it walked back inside to the rocks of the pages.

∽

In the future most books will be about Alfred Hitchcock; the point is that his films maximise both entropy and control.

∽

Aim straight for the small patch of desolation right at the heart of your politics.

∾

You were still talking underneath your voice about the salmon of knowledge, the ash tree chopped down by mysteries, and this is called poetry and it hurts like patience.

∾

In the photographs Artaud resembles nothing so much as a dirty iceberg, a fact that he referred to as absolute freedom.

∾

We were slumped inside the belly of history, pointing out whoever else we could see, as if we were really only windows.

∾

Would you like to be your own worst enemy or do you want a worse one to be out there somewhere?

∾

The dream was angrier with her than it had been since she first ate it.

∾

He could see the blood woven on the hands of the speeches; we all can.

∾

Global warming is a conspiracy and the air is in on it; the ghost of Karl Marx drifts in the trees like the voice of a pale dog.

~

You were a new sort of social class as you let the news track you down to every corner.

~

All the hours are anthropologists who have been sent down to watch our reactions.

~

You do not know why you are lying to me for that matter.

~

Earth sucks up all the lives wandering in space and turns them into us.

~

We shimmered outside the galleries like planets waiting to be colonised, the very darkness of the night had fled from our windows and plazas.

~

Margaret Thatcher was as raucous and effortless as any of the other great hits of the punk era.

~

No one there was hungry apart from the waiters.

~

It is not as if many of the options have so far been tried.

~

The skyscrapers in Chicago watched him without flinching, their faces were mordant about the light, and they knew how sad money needs to be in order to stay so strong.

∿

Maybe it really was a farce as Mark Zuckerberg was thrown the costume of Chairman Mao.

∿

Vallejo's mind had to move faster and faster to stay ahead of the needles of his fingers, the needles of the months as they clicked like tiny drums, the minds inside his mind and the ones inside them too.

∿

She had never seen anything more stupid than nature.

∿

The history of Tony Blair is the story of a smile taking a long time to understand that it is a form of panic.

∿

The traders were made of onyx on the inside, and slabs of rare types of marble, and they found it hard to breathe.

∿

We went in search of the secrets of the grains of light, and we found cinemas and sliding magazines, and popcorn splurging in the canisters like a host of little brains.

∿

In Birmingham the roads bristle and track one another like the hairs on the back of a donkey.

∾

It may be a streaming leaf or it may be the jaw of a monastic chant.

∾

You will have to pay in the future to find out what they mean by capitalism in the first place.

∾

You saw Shelley still seeing the face of murder and you split into two different people at least.

∾

All food carries a mystery and the memory of a gun; the sacred is a leaf slipping out of your face or your brain.

∾

It was easy to stand outside the wedding, without light, carrying an address book and a pile of melodies.

∾

Dancing had become a matter of sheer persistence, of grievance breaking itself up into fragments of law.

∾

The memory sat inside her like a gate at night, and then it was night, and she slept held by the hands of the air vents and the traffic.

～

Sappho threw all her fragments up in the air like the noises of a wedding or like guns or threads or birds.

～

It was time to say no to Joseph Cornell, it was time to let the pictures of parrots and the sugarcubes fly back into the wilderness.

～

In the future most television shows will be hosted by insects.

～

The lake of moonlight was wrestling with a long lake of darkness, as if the beauty of the sky fell from the hands of an athlete.

～

In the parable she broke all their legs one by one, and still called it creative writing.

～

It seems that we are still here after all; we shouted silently.

～

Miles Davis had to be both a hurricane and a murmur, if he wanted to survive at all.

～

How can anyone stay quiet beneath the gloomy wings of Blaise Pascal as they open and close like a skyline rummaging amongst office blocks and warehouses?

∾

A restaurant is just a tooth blown up to frantic proportions.

∾

At least Shakespeare will always be interested in you.

∾

It may make things only very slightly better if you get to exploit me too.

∾

The novel watched from the shelf and wondered what to say next about the walls of speech and chance.

∾

Homer stood and listened to the sea of his blindness, to the spear of his blindness, to the rush that he called the middle of things.

∾

Machiavelli knew that what we need is a centaur, and he had not even seen any John Wayne films.

∾

No one told the horses that they were in films; it is one of the things that poured a certain tautness into the skin of the westerns.

∾

You rolled the little dice of sleep in the hands of your breaths.

∾

It was like being larger than eyesight and more ornate; a woman steps out of a story and they have to find themselves, amidst hard waves and fallen villages.

∾

He did not know how to look for his eyes in the first place.

∾

You will be saved by the ground beneath your stampedes; the poems will study us in return, seeking the places where they might be able to build.

∾

Drizzle slid through the evening in pieces like the face of a prayer that brushes past you.

∾

Thomas Bernhard put his pride so deep inside his weakness in order to protect it.

∾

Antonioni is still waiting for you at the edge of the pictures, his face still fettered with sharp joy, his pain still whetting the ridges of beauty.

∾

We were so noisy and so veeringly silent.

∾

Two mountains were scaling each other amidst the waves of the sheets and the leavings of the day.

∾

Go as far away from yourself as possible, and then make yourself catch up so curtly that it hurts; the social problems too are longing to be understood.

∾

He was filming his life as it ensued, and every day he needed new cameras to film the ones that he had brought the day before.

∾

Air is breathing a long way inside you like an animal with soft teeth.

∾

The quest is for higher quality regrets.

∾

It will take you to the feet of the blood of the divine, no further really, although the shallow and loaded hills there will be your breaths.

The Further Adventures Of The Lives Of The Saints

Spinning out of the quick mildness of the afternoon, the lives
of the saints come by in floating procession,
and some of the lives of the saints are carrying
signboards with images of tongues, or sketches
of rambling, maddening desert vistas,
while others are wearing habits emblazoned with slogans
explaining the most intimate details of time's patience, or
joking about some new idea that some saint or other has had
about the wild spaces sloping between words and things,
the lives of the saints are smiling so smoothly that it does not
exactly reassure, but that may be what being beatific means,
something both total and outside of itself,
a sharpness sliding away inside the radiant surfaces,
now some of the lives of the saints are carrying the
peacefully sleeping heads of other saints,
and some are drinking blood as tenderly
as if it was the most raw tequila,
and some of them are intoning the formulas for
atomic fission, and some of the lives are now themselves
exploding, leaving little fragments of anecdotes or the memories
of images burning amongst the cloudscapes and the sumptuous bushes,
and then walking on as if they were revolving doors and still carrying
beautiful little bursts of loss in phials the size of
the tip of the tail of a scorpion or a very large thorn,
and hissing past like sails or hours or epochs.

∾

Jerome's lion streaks across the tawny afternoon like a story,
guarding the ass called truth as it brays and brays beside it.

∾

The lives of the saints have sometimes become reclusive,
in certain moods they barely even look at you,
whispering to themselves inside stones like woodlice
or burning slowly like the sounds of pain stuck
in the erosion at the bottoms of ponds,
waiting with the stark and dishevelled patience
of landfill, holding strict poses for years
within the ornate glare of the hard perspectives
of very early renaissance landscapes,
or opening and closing their mouths as they read like the sea
taking away its dark brilliance and then giving it
straight back beneath the vertigo of moonlight,
but revealing nothing, holding their ideas so close,
as if to insist that nothing has been decided
so far by anyone's powers of hearing.

           ∿

Later, you would see some of them riding in the early
evenings on packed underground trains,
their faces full of poise and density
on the way back from rehearsals or cleaning jobs or
the odd fairly small public meeting, their faces
smeared with bumpy ochre light, their faces
as soft as warm wax against the black air that presses against
the windows, and that howls with little patches of bright
anger like snow that has turned black overnight.

           ∿

Superfluity
wanders, the lives of the saints tack so close to pointlessness
sometimes that it is part of the point, we
assume, as when Macarius walks off into the
desert to do penance for months, the heat and
the coldness clattering together like teeth,
after a flea bit him and he squashed it,

and saw little drops of blood oozing
out of it, his own no doubt included, though
it is not clear how much any of this is why
he feels so bad about it, in time he comes back out
of the slow wind of his solitude
in any case covered in sores and bites.

∾

A few of the lives of the saints had started to read one
of Breton's surrealist manifestos during a hazy and extravagantly hot
    afternoon,
and one of the saints remembered the two
lions that had turned up to bury his corpse centuries
earlier, their stark
tenderness, violence
and sweetness wrapping
around each other like the light
tearing itself off from the brim of
a star's gravity, and soon the two lions were themselves
streaming across the head of the
bright sky,
and laughing
as fiercely as the start of winter when it wraps itself in the voices of crows.

∾

In fact the saints had always loved
disguises, it sometimes seems as if there was no point
being one unless you could be taken for something else entirely.

∾

Nothing is more quiet than oil
paint, it is greedy for the least hint of
quietness, it scrapes the last little jolts of it
out of the painter's mind and layers them into its

colours, or it reaches into the studio or,
years later, the gallery or the museum around it,
and snatches all the quietness that corners or eyesight
can harbour, it hoards it, the way a tree will pull all
the dimness that it can find out of the
evening, and pour it thirstily down amongst
the quiet flames of its limbs and leaves.

∾

Beneath the elegant strictures of a plane tree's heft and gauntness, the
lives of the saints are reading bits of the lives of the saints
aloud, and the city groans like a forest,
or fans out as fiercely as a hand of cards, stares
lovingly into its own strength like a weapon, while
the lives of the saints dilate,
vanish, and
remain.

∾

Eustace is not yet called Eustace when he follows
the stag that he is meant to be hunting
to a peak where it turns towards him,
in fact it is the usual reversal,
and the stag turns out to have been hunting him,
though reports differ
as to whether the voice comes out of the stag's own mouth,
or from the image of the cross that flashes
out from between the stag's antlers,
and you had indeed always been all too prone to looking
in two directions, at least.

∾

In Rossellini's film about Francis the rain sweeps down out of
the sky of the images with a gravity so wildly
relentless that it begins to feel like merriment, the monks
twist like tops to discover which way to
go, while in the Dreyer film about Joan of Arc the black and
white powder of the images whips on to
the saint's face and off her and she
redeems it by keeping her eyes more open even than the muscles
sharpening inside a
seagull's wings
as it climbs the castle of the air.

∾

While summer goes on falling as steadily as fruit, while
the heaven of despair goes on wandering amongst the tusks of
the faint rain clouds in the exalted and ranging evenings, a saint
is someone whose life is written in
words held all the way inside
a stone capable
of holding the eternal down for a moment or two.

∾

The life of a saint is a hosepipe
plugged into the flow of the eternal, the life of a saint glances out of
the window of a cave and sees a wolf handing a pig back to a widow of
    course.

∾

You need to learn how to get out
quickly, the lives of the saints will have messed us
up.

∾

Violent peace and hopefulness that glares as steadily
as honey, wisdom as loopy and repetitive as the gunfire in
action films, clownish sadness pressed hard into aching
faces, hunching cliffs, braced against
their own thoughts like torsos waiting for ecstasy,
sights breaking in different directions like sycamore
leaves, all the blindness inside the quick black water that hearing
becomes, and then a word like 'solitude'
scanning the rocks and waves like the beams from a
lighthouse, prayers like honey too in the way that they keep hold of
all their scorched heat somewhere deep inside, bleakness
waiting with all the sharp beauty of a bird calling
on the name of a saint to save itself from a hawk's pursuit,
the lives of the saints run inside all these thoughts like a pack of
wolves running inside their hunger and the scrolls
of dim air.

      ∿

Maybe the best tear in the world is the one falling
and not falling in a Carlo Dolci painting
in the Dulwich Picture Gallery from the tilting face of a
saint who looks outwards and down and away from the
faces of the viewers in the gallery where she hangs and
cries,
it is a sad little leaf jutting out of a tree of
ecstasy that you do not see, it shapes
itself as sweetly and sharply as the curves scratched
by moonlight in glassy water, you can see
in fact how slowly he worked, about the slowest
painter indeed that Italy had ever dreamed of, his hands
dipping in and out of the tiny tear as if it was a flame or
the fire of a wound, and now the whole of London is
lying outside with its face as massive as a lost language.

      ∿

The lives of the saints are machines
for processing strangeness,
it can be as stealthy as anorexia
or as rapid as a conversation with a bird on a
dishevelled pathway,
or it can be an ecstasy as hard and bland as a marble
column,
whatever it is,
a saint's life is full of
pulleys and girders for rearranging it, levers and
scraps
of code for sorting it through,
you watch a low wall destroying and rebuilding itself for hours,
the body is the electrical forest in which the spirit
wanders,
and now love is running in like the feet of morning light grasping slightly
wet gravel.

∾

Remember too the gawky pathos of all the small demons
as they scurry out of the lives of the saints and into the meaningless
rings, their faces like shirts being wrung out on a cliff top.

∾

The thirteen ways at least in which a blackbird might look at the life of a
saint are waiting
on the tip of the rooftop, and Kevin
too is sitting briefly on top of the evening, Silvester
explained once that the divine part survived the death on the cross in the
way that the sunlight thrown across a tree survives even if the tree is
shattered,
it is a fact that pain is
a friend,
you turn around and the day has closed its eyes and vanished, and nothing
but the truth about the heavens will return it.

∾

Indiscriminately
solid, the minds of the lives of the saints were mainly made of paper for a
while, now they are also made of various sorts of shimmering digital
dreck, the bursts on the other side of the pixels,
the figures shunting away inside
liquid crystal displays,
so you imagine, say, a collaborative
stack of webpages called the lives of the saints, of course,
to which anyone could contribute a story,
or a twist of imagery that would fall open like a cloud's mouth sucking in
moisture,
or that would stick an idea on like a sack of sand clasped to the back of a
    saint.

∾

Now the life of a saint is looking drowsy in the corner of a bar,
and it is also a gunslinger, ready to stop you in your tracks
but also happy to let its oldfashioned drawl amuse you.

∾

A day twists its eternal wheels like another shy
unicorn walking over the tapestry of the roofs of the terraces,
you have to learn not to try
to take the dirt out of the
silence,
the signposts and tables building like scurf and even the wild animal noises
    of the
hissing roads.

∾

Ambrose hurries away in the story
along with his retinue from the
lovely house
of the man who has just been telling
him that his life has always been entirely
prosperous,
and soon afterwards
the earth does indeed open up
and it swallows the man and his household down entirely,
leaving behind a ravine full of landscapes of air as empty
as the hands of Theresa as she reaches down and draws Bernini's
hands towards the hard river of the marble.

∾

You could think too of the in many ways distinctly unsaintly Claude
Lanzmann, as he kept on watching
as the holocaust kept talking in front of him like a train track.

∾

If you see a beautiful woman called pity in a dream,
her crown will be made of olive leaves,
as if charity means being extracted from the wrestling branches.

∾

You were nobody to begin with and you will be nobody in
the end, you know all this already of
course, the question is whether you can discover
a new structure for being nobody
in,
you turn all the houses into the lives of saints,
the city disappears,
and then the lives of the saints disappear too,
you know of course about how even heat itself is always
leaving,
and the wind growls beside the empty bed of the darkness.

～

The life of a saint simply blows onto the idol that it has been led to
so that it can be forced to sacrifice to it,
the thing crumbles like a breath,
and now it is years later, the lives
of the saints watch the lives of the ministers, and the lives
of the committees and the special advisors, and love them more than you
might think.

～

Anthony is in one of his ecstasies and sees the surface
of the earth covered in snares,
you might think that this is a fairly
standard otherworldly putdown,
but when he is asked how they can be avoided,
and humility is his answer,
since what humility means is in fact staying close
to the earth,
he seems to be saying that the answer to the problems
of the earth is to get closer
to it than you were before,
closer to the scabs of bent colour meditating on the glass of
the pavements or the mirrors of the civic dumps,
closer to the revelatory gunk of snail tracks,
you press your innumerable cones and pores up close
to the air's hard hands.

～

It is like finding a video of a wound slowly healing
and speeding it up until it looks absurd,
and then watching it again or again and again until
it starts to look both absurd and not,
the lives of the saints know more than newspapers or even meadows
about the ligatures of a world
in which torture and beauty start by merely staring at each other.

∾

The lives of the saints are also birds flying but bereft
of sense, rancid, wounded, tired, unreliable to the point where it gets
        boring,
jumpy, platitudinous, slack, morose, confused, in chains,
you may think that you know how repetitive they are going to
be, but they stubbornly find ways of being more so.

∾

You have to learn to be hungry
too, it is harder than they make it seem and more alive,
a cave ends up loving air more than itself
and sucks the
darkness ever further down into the
brains
of
the rocks
as slowly as part of a wafer flooding the end of your tongue,
you keep dreaming about old, almost forgotten
friends, and also about people that you have not even met
yet, and the lives of the saints sometimes only stick to you
in the ways that starlight manages to cling to the crazy, slender branches of
the night.

∾

It is not hunger that they overcome, it
is whatever keeps claiming to stand outside it,
and solitude too can be a meeting smeared with snatches of songs and
    flakes of neon light.

∾

The lives of the saints are pop
music videos, variants
on various lurid and fairly simple
drives, doves circle, implements of torture
gleam before melting, abbots ask themselves
who they really are and whether they can really be
forgiven, emperors drive past wearing gleaming
sunglasses, numberless are the grains of sand singing love songs with voices
softer than a drop of water clinging to a thorn's curvature.

∾

The same blue sky behind or over or around
the sharp lines of the heads of the lives of the saints is flayed with strands
of beauty, Bernard once had to excommunicate a horde of
flies, he learnt from the theology of oaks and beeches, but once walked
beside the lake at Lausanne without even noticing it,
in fact he lived for a whole year in the novices' cells without noticing
the vaulted ceiling, so it is clear that description
is not as important as we like to think, he stopped
himself from dwelling on some dazzling insight that he
had had, because he did not want to stop the next one from coming,
we read about the vanquishing of dragons and about fountains
of tears, but the bright tears were dragons too, devouring
the sad faces of the landscapes.

∾

To begin with no one even knew what the colours
would be, the lives of the saints had to
explain them one by one as the pigments and compounds
flowed, in fact this is what the much disputed concept
of the middle ages really comes down to.

       ∽

A fierce white star in the shape of a
sword hung for a year over the city of
the lives of the saints with all
its bristling herb gardens and its bright
fragments of
limbs,
it stopped history dead in its tracks as if
it was a poisonous berry or a
padlocked heart,
or at least it yearned so deeply to do so that even the sea of history
gasped
as it washed its face in the streams of the night.

       ∽

Throw all your losses in piles at the ground like wet leaves,
drink the day even if it tastes like medicine,
and watch how a bridge keeps walking over the
torment of a small river endlessly,
daily,
it walks across on its own back like a language,
it looks downwards at time and upwards at the eternal
lives
of the air,
the lives of the saints are watching you
as intensely as a weather front watches a ridge of
clouds,
you may not be completely happy about it,
you may wish that they would explain what is strict and what is tender,

the sky curves like the mind with no other
structure than the edges of sheer joy,
and water wanders in loops through the raindrops and the caverns like a
brain,
and art is full of hints like a small fire writing its name in smoke and
    broken flames.

Strain

Somewhere in between the thought that there is no truth anywhere
and the idea that all men are equal,
a poem is being written,
it is being written over and over again with the relentlessness of a train
    passing
smoothly over its tracks and eating them one by one,
poems like trains need to have good digestions,
and the train gets through incalculable miles like a mountain drinking up
rainfall, it flares like a match against a dismal horizon,
it moves through the soluble ochre haze of a suburban evening,
through the vertigo of radio waves and the fecklessness of drizzle,
it goes past the crowds of leaves sleeping in the heads of the trees and it
    does not
think about them or about anything except you and how it can find you,
and it does not even know what it should call you,
because the truth is that it is not a train and in fact it is not really a poem
    either,
after all, no one likes poetry that only refers to itself,
it is more like the reflection of an iron bridge in one of the train's dark
    windows,
or maybe like the fused light held in the rainwater grasped by a thorn
a bit earlier in the same day,
or a wounded path where shards of grass are growing new bodies,
new flesh for your brain to contemplate one day,
or to eat,
one way or another it has become something else already,
and has gone right past you to somewhere where it can love you more
    fluently,
the little word 'you' on which all our worlds must balance.

ℂB editions

Founded in 2007, CB editions publishes chiefly short
fiction (including work by Will Eaves, Gabriel Josipovici,
David Markson and May-Lan Tan) and poetry (Beverley
Bie Brahic, Nancy Gaffield, J. O. Morgan, D. Nurkse,
Dan O'Brien). Writers published in translation include
Apollinaire, Andrzej Bursa, Joaquín Giannuzzi, Gert
Hofmann, Agota Kristof and Francis Ponge.

Books can be ordered from www.cbeditions.com.